Esprit de Corps

GUIDING PRINCIPLES
& SPIRITUALITY
FOR MODERN
MARINE TEAMS

JOANNA MENDOZA

BALBOA.
PRESS

A DIVISION OF HAY HOUSE

Balboa Press books may be ordered through booksellers or by contacting:

Balboa Press
A Division of Hay House
1663 Liberty Drive
Bloomington, IN 47403
www.balboapress.com
1 (877) 407-4847

Because of the dynamic nature of the Internet, any web addresses or
links contained in this book may have changed since publication and
may no longer be valid. The views expressed in this work are solely those
of the author and do not necessarily reflect the views of the publisher,
and the publisher hereby disclaims any responsibility for them.

The author of this book does not dispense medical advice or prescribe the use
of any technique as a form of treatment for physical, emotional, or medical
problems without the advice of a physician, either directly or indirectly. The
intent of the author is only to offer information of a general nature to help you
in your quest for emotional and spiritual well-being. In the event you use any
of the information in this book for yourself, which is your constitutional right,
the author and the publisher assume no responsibility for your actions.

Any people depicted in stock imagery provided by Thinkstock are models,
and such images are being used for illustrative purposes only.
Certain stock imagery © Thinkstock.

Print information available on the last page.

ISBN: 978-1-5043-8102-4 (sc)
ISBN: 978-1-5043-8103-1 (e)

Library of Congress Control Number: 2017908098

Balboa Press rev. date: 05/24/2017

Contents

Dedication

To those who walked before me, who lit the flame;
To those who walk beside me, that guards the flame;
And to those, in the future,
Who will keep the flame lit
For generations to come.

Preface

I N 1999 I JOINED THE Marine Corps, after serving in the United States Navy for three years, under the apprenticeship program. The military has been my life for over twenty years. After retiring, I felt it was important to share what I have learned along the way. Since I can no longer lead as an active-duty marine, this book is my attempt to directly impact a generation of marines who have the ability to affect change, to take things back to the basics. When I enlisted, marines polished their boots and ironed their uniforms. Our uniforms were stiffly starched, so that they made a crinkling sound when we walked. Tattoos were acceptable. Non-judicial punishment was proof you had joined the ranks as a real marine. And word[1] was passed in formation.

The company gunny was the most inspirational marine in the unit. You know the type—prior drill instructor who spoke with his hands. Every time he talked to you, he aimed loaded knife hands at your face. He rocked a high and tight and said the words "freaking" and "daggon." The company gunny told fascinating stories and drank a pot of black coffee every day. He had 101 reasons why marines are awesome and bragged about why the Marine Corps is the most elite fighting force in the world. We considered him "the keeper of the flame."

The keeper of the flame wasn't just reserved for prior drill

---

[1]   Information on daily tasks, events, and activity passed to troops, usually by the platoon sergeant.

instructors. It could be any marine who carried a heart shaped into an eagle, globe, and anchor. I considered myself a keeper of the flame. I vowed to protect our legacy through continued practice of our corps' traditions, customs, and courtesies. I taught young marines about traditions and showed them how to foster a passion for who we are and what we do. I told colorful tales of the past, passionate stories of warriors that went before us. And in doing so, I instilled a deeper sense of pride and ownership.

It's not enough to assume that marines will research our history on their own. We must inspire them to do so, in order to keep the flame lit. Something magical happens when we share stories about our legacy. It shows that we value the lessons learned from our corps' illustrious history and that we will never forget.

It is my deepest wish that you share the contents of this book, in order to strengthen our connections to each other and nourish the spirit of our beloved Marine Corps. Maintaining this connection has become part of our life source and illuminates the path we walk as marine warriors.

Enjoy the magic contained within.

One team, one fight!

Big Momma Gunz

Acknowledgments

W ITH MUCH GRATITUDE AND ADMIRATION, thank you all for continuing to believe in me.

Mom-Anna Villar	Dad-Jose Mendoza	Senaida Valdivia
Egnacio Valdivia	Rosie Mendoza	MGySgt Justin Aiken
Maj Katherine Spicer	Col. James Clark	Maj Marco Campos
GySgt P. Rowell (Ret.)	Maj David Keele (Ret.)	1stSgt Julia Vetos (Ret.)
1stSgt O. Leavy	SgtMaj Courvielle (Ret.)	Col. Brett Bourne
Capt. Daniel Fetsch	Sgt Edina Tellez	Sgt Rocio Sanchez
Maj Minor	LtCol Erika Cashin	GySgt Neil Absalon
1stSgt Jackie Muncy	GySgt Christine Hitzing	1stSgt Michelle Macea
1stSgt Elba Estremera	2ndLt Jessica Barnes	Maj B. Braun
Salvador Jr. Valdivia	Anna Maria Valdivia	Maj Jessica Karlin
SSgt Jody Danks (Ret.)	1stSgt Chris Rivera	GySgt Victor Ortiz
Capt. Ashford	SgtMaj Michael Cato	GySgt Beth Abbott
GySgt Jessica Wysote	GySgt T. Nelson (Ret.)	GySgt Shantee Williams
SgtMaj Sean Greenleaf	SgtMaj Vizcarrando	SgtMaj R. Rodriguez

Introduction

S OME PEOPLE LEARN ABOUT TEAMWORK during high school, while participating in sports; others learn about team concepts at after-school clubs and programs; and some don't learn about teamwork at all until they're forced to on the job. The United States Marine doesn't necessarily start out as a perfect team member operating in unity. The understanding is shaped and molded in boot camp. Soon after arriving on the yellow footprints at Marine Corps Recruit Depot (Parris Island or San Diego), recruits find themselves stripped of individuality. There is no "I" in "team"!

By the third phase, we expect recruits to understand that they won't make it without the recruit to the left or right of them. Additionally, by this point recruits understand that the lack of cohesion on a team can jeopardize the life of everyone on it—or at least get them quarter decked for now. Pain retains; it is better to experience it on the quarterdeck for 3-30 and 3^2 than on the battlefield, bleeding out.

Teamwork is essential for any team, but the teamwork concept doesn't always guarantee success. There are other variables that will predict if a team will be successful, and the Marine Corps does a great job at instilling the warrior mentality within its ranks. The framework is put into each marine individually and then weaved into the team

---

[2]   "3-30 and 3" stands three minutes, thirty seconds, and three minutes, which is the length of the retention/disciplinary technique known as incentive training (IT).

in boot camp by the drill instructor team. Drill instructors are the epitome of a team operating in perfect unison and the first model of a team for the platoon. Each member on the team is trained for the mission of making marines. Additionally, each member has a specific role, with a specific set of responsibilities that are co-dependent on the next.

A member's every move is calculated, to the point where they can anticipate the actions of the members on their team. Because competency is an important part of the drill instructor team, they are constantly adjusting based on the outcome. Success isn't measured by how much revenue the marines brought in that quarter; it's literally measured on a scale of life or death.

If not trained properly, the new marine will enter the operating forces and become a burden. That burden could literally cause someone his or her life. Boot camp instills a greater sense of accountability to each individual and the organization. The marine's primal instinct is to protect the marine to the left or right of them.

The marine team dynamic is unique. The combination of pride, competence, and a firm belief in each other, and in something greater than oneself, gives marines a competitive edge in the teamwork department. This quality is hard to replicate, especially in a society that has become far removed from any concept that might lend itself to spirituality.

How to Use This Book

T HIS BOOK IS TO BE used as a guide to reinforce unity and pride in your team. Additionally, it can be used as a way to strengthen the bond among individuals within your unit. Selected chapters provide guiding principles and tools to create lasting connections. The information contained within this book is most useful to young marine leaders, but it can benefit more expired leaders, as well, especially, if they are looking for new ideas on team building.

To get the most from this book, I've added a few recommendations:

+ *Take notes. Keep a journal or a small notebook.* Write directly in the book or in your designated notebook. A leader should always carry something to write on and write with.

+ *Encourage participation from other marines in your section.* When reading any book, share what you're reading with others. I've been doing this for years. Reading a book concurrently with someone else not only makes great conversation, but it will also allow you to actually finish the book—especially since getting most young marines to read is like pulling teeth from a lion's mouth.

+ *Encourage weekly group discussions.* Holding weekly mentorship meetings is a great way to exchange information. Additionally, it serves to keep momentum on projects, such as assigned reading, which I know every marine loves. (wink)

- *Stay on topic.* Before the weekly discussion, send out information regarding the meeting, the five W's (who, what, where, when, why,) and the how. Create an agenda, and send it out via email, so marines know what to expect in the meeting. Who likes going to meetings that are unorganized and lengthy. Not only is it irritating, but it's easy to lose interest. Addressing what the marines will need to bring or topics they should be prepared to talk about will keep your meeting on schedule. And don't be late to your own meeting.
- *Be consistent.* Good habits don't develop overnight. Read every day, even if it's a few pages.
- *Complete all the exercises contained therein.* Before continuing to the next chapter, complete any exercises contained in that chapter. Like most processes, if you skip a step, it can affect the results.
- *Be honest in your answers.* Most likely, you'll be sharing your opinions and thoughts with others in your section. Don't say something because you think it's what others want to hear. Chances are, people will be able to tell you're lying. That is not a great way to build trust, which is essential in a team.

CHAPTER 1

Corporate Corps

THE SECOND CONTINENTAL CONGRESS ORDERED the creation of two battalions, and the first marines enlisted on November 10, 1775, led by Captain Samuel Nicholas. Although 1775 is often considered the year when the marines were born, they came into existence long before that. The first marines were recruited in 1740 and known as Gooch's Marines. They were named after the first (unofficial) commandant of the Marine Corps, Colonel William Gooch. They served on British ships with the Royal Marines during the French and Indian War.

Gooch's Marines were more than three thousand men strong. They volunteered to fight aboard British ships from various states along the East Coast, such as New York, New Jersey, New England, Pennsylvania, Delaware, Maryland, Virginia, and North Carolina. These men didn't come from well-to-do families, nor did they possess an ivy league education. The men stepped forward to protect a divided union, not because they possessed a sense of duty to their nation, but because they were poverty stricken, from the slums, and had tiny mouths to feed. Volunteering to be a marine was the last effort to provide basic necessities for their families. But in most historical literature, they are depicted as criminals, looters, thieves, and homeless vermin who lacked moral character. I find it difficult to believe men lacking moral character would be the first volunteering to sacrifice their lives. Maybe they were actually good men who just happened to be poor. Nonetheless, they fought because they had to live. Not much has changed since then. It appears that those from lower socioeconomic backgrounds are often the first to sacrifice their lives for a cause.

Colonel Gooch led marines under the Forty-Third American Regiment of Foot from 1740 to 1742. British Marines trained Gooch's Marines on shipboard duties, ship-to-shore operations, small arms fire, and ship's gun training. These men hoped that upon returning they would have gained valuable skills to make a fair living and be able support their families.

Many of Gooch's Marines didn't survive the deployment because of tropical diseases, mainly yellow fever. Out of the three thousand men who originally volunteered, a little more than three hundred (seventeen officers, thirteen noncommissioned officers, and 286 sick enlisted marines) returned, some with illnesses that eventually led to their deaths. The first institution of marines was short-lived. In October 24, 1742, the Forty-Third American Regiment was disbanded, pushing Gooch's surviving men to serve under other regiments. Although they were instrumental, they were considered dispensable assets.

It's safe to assume that during this time the Marine Corps lacked structure and standards because there was not a need to keep the marines around. It wasn't until after the American Revolution that the founders focused on establishing a Marine Corps that was high in demand. Gooch's Marines are a strong reminder that in order to take care of our marines, we must establish strong values and guide them to find purpose, individually and as a team. Ignoring these tasks will lead to the destruction of our Marine Corps, just like the plague wiped out Gooch's Marines.

The chances of our current Marine Corps being wiped out by a plague such as yellow fever may seem unlikely, but there is a plague out there that has the potential to destroy the organization. It lurks in the shadows and has been slowly infecting our marines. I call it the corporate plague.

When I first joined, the Marine Corps functioned and acted like a family. It was a people-first culture. We placed emphasis on accomplishing the mission and adhering to tradition, but taking care of the marines was always the priority. "Mission first, marines always!" Marines took care of each other. Those days have nearly faded away; the marine warrior is seen as expendable rather than the nation's most valuable asset.

It's important to understand that in the beginning, the Marine Corps was born out of necessity. Today, the American people want a Marine Corps. However, throughout the years, it has transformed into a corporation that favors a stone-cold professional image over compassion and empathy for its service members. It has become cold and corporate.

What Is Corporate Corps?

Corporate corps is a hybrid of corporate mind-set and Marine Corps structure that cares more about image than taking care of its people. The corporate corps mentality creates the illusion of a culture of teamwork and values that make marines believe they are a part of something bigger than themselves. But it's a lie. Control measures are implemented, disguised as directives, with claims of creating a better establishment for all. The reality is that these control measures serve the personal and political agenda of those we view as our fearless leaders.

Disciplinary issues throughout the Marine Corps have skyrocketed as a result of this corporate mind-set. A corporate culture leaves no room for inspiration or creativity. It creates marines who are afraid to make decisions; for fear that they will fail or make a mistake. Zero-defect mentality is in full effect. The Marine Corps I grew up in wanted leaders who acted respectfully and morally, understanding that people make mistakes. Instead, the decision makers think they can fix our disciplinary issues by implementing stricter guidelines or deterrent programs designed to scare marines straight. The overwhelming amount of dos and don'ts, disguised as higher standards, has resulted in untrusting and resentful marines.

In the last decade, the "big, green, lean, mean fighting machine" has been hit hard by the corporate plague. It didn't come from the private first class, as the hierarchy makes you believe. Senior leadership has been selling the notion that our disciplinary issues are due to a generation of marines who don't want to work hard and refuse to be disciplined. Don't believe it!

America's youth is sometimes rebellious, but it's that rebellious spirit that makes America great. It isn't our young marines who have infected the Marine Corps. Our issues didn't start at the bottom of our ranks. Junior marines aren't the culprits of the corporate plague; sphere of influence is.

Junior marines don't have a huge sphere of influence; they might have influence on one or two other marines. Maybe it's middle management (meaning sergeants)? Think again. Sergeants can only make decisions that affect the marines under their charge. The culprits are senior leaders who have the most influence on the masses. They have influence on policy and make policy.

The corporate plague began at the top and has been making its way down the ranks, breeding a generation of heartless leaders that will devour everything in their path that doesn't serve their selfish interests. It continues to spread like cancer within our ranks. If we don't stop the infestation, in a few decades, we won't recognize the Marine Corps. The first step in curing the corporate plague is to understand what causes it.

Causes

As a leader, it can be difficult to find a balance in doing what's right for the organization and what's right for the marine. Mastery often comes with some trial and error. This is why it's important that we promote leaders at a rate that allows them to gain experience in managing a variety of issues. Early promotions perpetuate the cycle of leaders who don't know how to handle personnel issues. And if you aren't confident in tending to the needs of your marines, those needs are often neglected in the hope that the problem will just go away. But the problems don't go away; they snowball. Before you know it, you have marines showing up late for work, neglecting their hygiene, and being less productive. It's important to understand that the plague didn't happen overnight. There are several factors that can lead to or increase the risks: excessive deployment schedules or workloads, early promotions, lack of professional and personal development, lack of recognition, and lack of empathy and understanding.

Excessive Deployment Schedules or Workloads

Marines who put in excessive hours often end up feeling unappreciated. Mission accomplishment overshadows productivity and efficiency. Leaders get wrapped up in getting the job done (at any cost) and don't take a moment to appreciate how much time and effort their marines have taken in getting the job done, and getting it done right.

Early Promotions

I am not a big fan of meritorious promotions and definitely not a fan of book boards. When selecting marines to go on meritorious boards, the book should be only one part of the equation. Before the board even goes, leaders should have months observing the marine's performance, character, and level of maturity, not to mention how well they deal with confrontation and conflict. Additionally, leaders should pay special attention to why a marine believes he or she earned the next rank. The last thing I want to hear is that they want to make more money, do less work, or tell others what to do. They should want to get promoted because they want to be an advocate for the needs of those they lead.

Lack of Professional and Personal Development

Enlisted marines don't have enough opportunities for professional education. Professional Military Education (PME) isn't enough to give our leaders the tools they need to effectively lead others. This is part of the problem with the corporate mind-set. Those in power continue to gain knowledge and advance and keep the masses uneducated and stagnant.

Lack of Empathy and Understanding

The zero-defect mentality has junior marines believing that they aren't allowed to fail or make mistakes. Mistakes and failure are essential for development and growth. When marines believe that there isn't a way to overcome adversity, especially in their own lives, it perpetuates negativity and depression.

If we don't know how to identify what plagues our marines, then we can't come up with viable solutions to address the issues. Identification and acceptance are the first steps.

CHAPTER 2

Identifying the Plague

T HERE ARE ALWAYS SYMPTOMS THAT develop when a disease is present. You might not see the symptoms at first, as your body is doing everything (internally) to fight the infestation. But eventually, the indication that you are sick begins to surface and the illness reveals its ugly head. When you get a cold, your nose begins to run, you run a fever, and begin to feel achy. It's the same thing with the corporate plague. There are indicators that you can look for to identify it before it begins the hostile takeover.

Take a month to observe your surroundings and take notes. If safety is involved, however, take action right away. Begin by

- observing the area: Is it clean? Is there neglected equipment?
- observing the marines: Are their uniforms clean? Grooming?
- observing behavior: Are they happy? Smiling? Joking?
- observing the leadership: Are they present? How do they interact with their marines?

Observing the Area

To start, take a look around. Look at your work area. How clean is it? Does all of the equipment function? When I first came back to the operating forces after being on the drill field for three years,

7

the first thing I noticed at my new unit was how dirty it was. The parking lots and trash bins surrounding the gate were covered in trash. The office was filled with computer monitors, keyboards, and an old copying machine that didn't work. The marines kept their desk semi-clean, but wires dangled from their desks and surge protectors were daisy-chained.

Walking through the compound on my way to the S4 office, I stopped dead in my tracks when I came across what appeared to be a junkyard for equipment—right in the middle of the compound! I couldn't believe it. I walked through the junkyard, only to find more discarded office equipment. It was obvious that marines used the equipment to take out their frustration, because it was abused: 20-foot COMM shelters with graffiti, a cannibalized 7-ton, crates filled with ammo brass, the list goes on. It was horrific. The worst part was that the officer responsible for facilities, maintenance, and safety refused to do anything about it once it was brought to his attention. Knowing it wasn't right, I was forced to take action and drafted a report that eventually made its way to the commanding officer. Within a month the junkyard disappeared.

Observing the Marines

First impressions matter, and you only get one. If the first impression you get is neglect, be prepared to see more of it on all levels. Normally, if an area is not kept, then you will see marines who are unkempt as well. You'll most likely notice uniform violations, such as marines walking around in boots and uts, without covers, or dirty uniforms. Be advised, this will be just the beginning. Imagine the layers you will have to pull back to uncover the personal issues that the marines have.

Observing the Behavior

Negative behavior can spread like wildfire, especially if it's not identified and eliminated rapidly. If the section or unit has a high number of unauthorized absences, loss of creativity and productivity, or low morale, you may be seeing signs of the plague. High turnover rates can also be another indicator that there is an issue with the section or unit. Once marines realize that there is some negative juju, it isn't long before they try to find ways out. That is, if they know what's good for their careers. These marines know and understand that units with increased disciplinary issues will decrease their opportunities for advancement. They will volunteer for deployments and TAD positions or contact their monitors to get out while they still can. This isn't the right thing to do either. If you notice that marines walk around with their heads down, move slowly, or don't give the proper greeting of the day, this can be an indicator that morale is low. Marines, who love what they do move and have a sense of purpose, are unafraid to look into the eyes of others.

Observing the Leadership

Leaders with a people-first mentality focus where it matters: on the individual. Organizations with this culture understand that the survival of the organization depends on the individual to cultivate the culture. The welfare of the Marine comes first, as well as that of their families. People-first leaders make it a point to get to know their people outside of work and welcome meaningful feedback that improves processes. Tradition is still very much a part of the culture. Emphasizing the importance of knowing where we came from helps define who we are and what we represent.

Corporate corps leaders are extremists when it comes to traditions, picking and choosing traditions that support their personal agendas. And they definitely don't like input from their subordinates. The priority is the mission, and marines come second. Change is often difficult to embrace because they cling to antiquated concepts. The motto for this type of leadership is "Why change it if it isn't broken?" The corporate mentality is about advancing through the ranks for selfish reasons and not about advocating for their junior marines. Corporate corps leaders implement rules that reduce the decisions a small unit leader can make. The organizational culture is based on upholding unrealistic expectations.

CHAPTER 3

Spirit of the Body

OUR BELOVED MARINE CORPS' SPIRIT has been neglected in the last couple decades of war. The Marine Corps has consistently been deployed to combat zones since the initial push into Baghdad in 2003. We have gotten away from what distinguishes the corps from any other branch of service. The disregard for our marines and their spirituality has contributed to this deteriorated state. Politics and societal norms have caused us to get away from embracing our spirit, individually and as an organization.

But how do we except a generation of marine warriors to embrace spirit when they have been so far removed from the concept? How do we do this without compromising their foundational belief systems? Furthermore, why does this matter?

For over 243 years, the Marine Corps has remained alive by protecting its legacy. Because the Marine Corps is a spirit-based organization, its warriors recognize they have been called to serve a higher purpose. However, these days, the mere mention of spirituality in the Marine Corps rattles some people to the core. It may even keep some from fully embracing some of our time-honored traditions as marines. Nonetheless, the message of spirituality is weaved into our heritage and will continue to resonate within the corps. We must accept it and embrace spirit.

What Is Esprit De Corps?

The term used to describe camaraderie among military troops is "esprit de corps" (pronounced "espree de core"). Esprit de corps originated in France in the late eighteenth century and means "spirit of the body" or "group spirit."

Esprit de corps is defined by the following description: "the 'spirit' of a unit is commonly reflected by all members. It implies devotion and loyalty to the Marine Corps with deep regard for its history, traditions, and honor. It's the epitome of pride in the unit."

The common definition of esprit de corps is, "a feeling of pride, fellowship, and common loyalty shared by the members of a particular group."

The revised Marine Corps definition of esprit de corps is, "a feeling of immense pride and camaraderie reflected by members of an organization that implies loyalty and respect for the Marine Corps, with deep regard for history, tradition, and honor."

Where Did It Come From?

In 1918, more than thirty thousand marines served in France, which included the 5th and 6th Marine Regiments, who were awarded the French Fourragère and the Croix de Guerre (Cross of War) for heroic and gallant actions in combat. It is believed that the term came from France by marines who served there. The actions of those marines are some of the earliest examples of esprit de corps, as evident in the earliest published reference of the term in a *Marine Corps Gazette* article, titled "Esprit de Corps."[3]

---

[3]   Handsley, S. 1921. Esprit de Corps. September 1921, Volume 6, Issue 3. *Marine Corps Gazette*. https://www.mca-Marines.org/gazette/1921/09/esprit-de-corps.

Where Does It Begin?

Long before the Marine Corps officially adopted the corps' core values of honor, courage, and commitment, the value system was based on camaraderie and morale. Values like loyalty, sense of duty and responsibility, and integrity and characteristics like obedience, willpower, courage, and discipline are required of marines. The Marine Corps also requires that marines demonstrate teamwork as an essential character trait. Individuals who join often share common values and a love for country that calls them to a life of service to our great nation. You didn't just join the Marine Corps; you accepted the challenge and earned the privilege to call yourself a marine. And the spirit of the "lean, mean, green fighting machine" was instilled in you in boot camp.

Drill instructors develop the platoon's esprit de corps by exposing the team to a set of implicit principles that form the foundation of how the organization works. These rules are essential for the survival of any organization, but most importantly to the survival of the recruit and platoon as a whole.

What Do We Do to Fix It?

The issues our youth face today are battles within: the battle between good and evil. Only through understanding the issues can we find solutions that embrace wholeness and acceptance. There isn't a cookie cutter answer to address these issues on a mass level. We cannot secure our place as the nation's most elite fighting force if we do not intensify the spirit of the warrior first. The foundation must be purified from within.

Guiding Principles

After the recruit has earned the title of marine, they must continue to reinvigorate their soul, individually and as a team, in order to strengthen the essence of the corps. The principles that will help guide you to creating a team that is connected are:

+ Establish team size, structure, and roles.
+ Get to know your team.
+ Define the culture, value system, and function of your team.
+ Educate your team on organizational origins.
+ Determine how the team will identify themselves.
+ Test your teams' competence.
+ Keep your team inspired.

Major General John A. Lejeune, 13th Commandant of the Marine Corps

> This high name of distinction and soldierly repute we who are marines today have received from those who preceded us in the Corps. With it we have also received from them the eternal spirit, which has animated our Corps from generation to generation and has been the distinguishing mark of the Marines in every age. So, long as that spirit continues to flourish, Marines will be found equal to every emergency in the future as they have been in the past, and the men of our nation will regard us as worth successors to the long line of illustrious men who have served as "Soldiers of the Sea" since the founding of the Corps.[4]

---

[4] General John A. Lejeune's birthday message is required to be read at every Marine Corps birthday.

CHAPTER 4

Establish Team Size and Structure

A S MARINES, WE LEARN THE basics on team size and structure in boot camp. We are assigned to different sizes of teams within the platoon. We're taught that we can't go anywhere alone, and so we are assigned a battle buddy. This allows us to develop trust in those to the left and right of us. And as we know, everything (including trust) is earned, never given. It's important that a solid foundation is built from the start. One way to do this is to revert back to the basics.

Your platoon in boot camp is a great place to reference when establishing the size, structure, and roles of your team. For example, if you take a look at the team dynamic of your drill instructor team, most teams range between three to four. Occasionally, you will see a five-hat (drill instructor) team.[5] The drill instructor team is designed to be small for a reason, and the reason is that there are designated roles: the senior drill instructor, who acts as a voice of reason and father/mother figure; the "heavy," or "drill-hat," who is responsible for teaching recruits drill; the "knowledge-hat," who teaches recruits basic Marine Corps knowledge; and finally, the drill instructor, also known as the "kill-hat," who is responsible for discipline.

Size, structure, and roles are what keep complete chaos

---

[5] By the way, never call a Drill Instructor a "hat" if you've never been one.

from taking over. Additionally, designated roles have designated responsibilities, which prevents burnout, because one person isn't expected to do it all. We call this teamwork.

In a study conducted by Maximilien Ringelmann, a French engineer born in 1861, he concluded that the more people on a rope, the less individual effort was contributed. The ideal team size to prevent social loafing (the phenomenon of a person exerting less effort to achieve a goal when they work in a group than when they work alone) was determined to be between five to nine people. The Marine Corps uses the concept of breaking down groups into smaller ones, and the ideal size for a small footprint is usually a squad size or smaller.

The Marine Corps has always done more with less. Social loafing, also known as the Ringelmann Effect, explains why the Marine Corps has been able to adopt the "more with less" motto. In 2012 the Marine Corps was asked to put together a unit designed to retrograde all of the equipment out of Afghanistan. The commandant of the Marine Corps selected Colonel James Clark to command the unit in Afghanistan. He also happened to be my commanding officer at the time. I was proud to have been selected to be part of Colonel Clark's dream team and Marine Corps history.

The retrograde and redistribution in support of the reset and redeployment operations group, also known as the R4OG, was comprised of marines from units throughout the Marine Corps. R4OG was just over three hundred strong. This small unit was responsible for preparing, packaging, and shipping all Marine Corps assets; currently forward deployed back to CONUS. This was something that had not been done since the Korean War.

When the military packed up and left Iraq to go to Afghanistan, tons of equipment worth millions of dollars was left behind. Not only was it a waste of taxpayer money, but these assets could be collected by the enemy and used against us later. Being the good stewards that we are, the Marine Corps figured out how to get our equipment out of theater, so that other branches of service, such as the army, could mirror our operations.

What is unique about Colonel Clark's marines is that they came from so many different units and yet they were able to come together to complete the mission. Proving, once again, that we get more done with less every time. But this is what we expect of our marines—it's the standard. We expect them to step into any situation and adapt accordingly. But that's only part of the equation. We also need good leaders to carry out the Commander's intent. Appointed leaders have to delicately balance mission accomplishment and caring for marines in order to achieve the desired effect.

> For the strength of the pack is the wolf
> and the strength of the wolf is the pack.
> —Rudyard Kipling, *The Jungle Book*

Building the Wolf Pack

To date, one of my favorite recruiting posters was that of a marine who was half marine and half wolf. The quote on the poster said, "Think you have what it takes to be a Marine? Join the pack and find out." It was relevant then, and I find it still to be true. We consider ourselves to be part of a pack—a wolf pack that is fierce in battle and gentle when needed. Additionally, the bottom of the poster quoted Rudyard Kipling's book, *The Jungle Book*: "Now this is the law of the jungle—as old and as true as the sky; and the wolf that shall keep it may prosper, but the wolf that shall break it must die. As the keeper that girdles the tree-trunk. The law runneth forward and back. For the strength of the pack is the wolf; and the strength of the wolf is the pack."

Characteristics of the Wolf

Quiet	Compassionate	Confident	Protective
Adapts to the environment.		Possesses keen instincts and senses	
Values cooperation over competition		Respects elders	
Adheres to the wolf pack dynamics		Teaches the young	

+ *Size.* The size of your team is going to depend upon a few variables: your military occupational specialty and unit. Some military occupational specialties (MOS) operate in small groups—for example, intelligence and administrative shops. There are few things that you want to consider before assigning battle buddies and fire teams: experience, strengths, and shortcomings.

+ *Structure.* Before you assign all your star players on the dream team, ensure that you have a good mixture of experience. Additionally, you want to ensure that the marines you assign as battle buddies and fire team understand your reasons. Marines should know who is on their team. Sitting down with the assigned fire teams or squads and explaining the team dynamics and the method behind your madness will reduce resistance and complaining. Additionally, make it a habit to quiz team members about the whereabouts of those on their team, so that they can get used to checking in and out with each other. If you do this in garrison, it will reduce your accountability issues on deployments. Lastly, let them know that no one is above checking out. Model the behavior you want to see by letting your marines know where you are going.

+ *Roles.* Roles matter. Without roles, the efficiency and productivity is drastically reduced. Each member on the team should have assigned primary duties. Additionally, ensure that you assign assistants to major billet holders. This will not only give your more junior marines an opportunity to lead, but it will also prevent balls from being dropped. Assigned leaders should always be aware of commander's intent, in addition to the mission. Your team should understand how every level in the unit contributes to the mission.

Wolf Pack Dynamics (Chain of Command)

+ *Alpha*: Leader of the pack. For a fire team, this is the corporal or the senior lance corporal. For a squad, this is the sergeant or the senior corporal. In a platoon, this is the staff sergeant or senior sergeant.
+ *Alpha's Mate or Alpha A/*: Not applicable, as marines discourage this among team members. However, you could assign this to be the marine that is the alpha's right hand man or A/[6].
+ *Betas*: Trusted ones of the alphas. In a squad these are the fire team leaders.
+ *Subordinates*: Other squad members
+ *Omega*: Normally this is considered the weak link in the pack, but since marines don't have weaknesses (we have shortcomings), this is the most junior person on the team.

A fire team consists of alpha, alpha A/, beta, and omega. A squad consists of alpha, alpha A/, beta (fire team leaders), subordinates, and omega. A platoon consists of the same members as a squad, but betas will be squad leaders. As leaders, we may not always have the luxury of selecting our team. We are often thrown into situations that require our immediate attention, and we are expected to make miracles. Take a deep breath, and remember that you were placed in a position of special trust for a reason; help is always just a question away.

---

[6] The assistant billet holder is known as the A/.

CHAPTER 5

Get to Know Your Team

W E'RE IN THE BUSINESS OF winning hearts and minds everywhere we go. As a team leader, it's important to know who your marines are and where they came from. Backgrounds can be helpful, especially when dealing with disciplinary issues. Knowing where people came from gives you a better understanding of how they work and what they believe. The more time you spend in this organization, you will notice similarities between marines, allowing you to identify potential issues early on.

Your marines should also know a little bit about you and where you come from. Just as you develop opinions about your subordinates, they will develop opinions about you. It could prevent disciplinary issues and grievances against you.

Marines want to see your humanity. In fact, it makes you approachable. Marines don't want to seek guidance from someone who's uptight. They prefer to talk to someone who can relate to their issues, someone who is more like them. In telling them your personal story, you also help develop their emotional intelligence. Keep in mind that someday they will replace you in the ranks.

Exercise: Share Your Personal Story

Everyone has had to overcome obstacles in in life. Sometimes the obstacles are big. Sometimes they are small, but they exist. Our personal stories often involve painful memories that we'd like to forget, but had we not experienced them, we may not be where we are today.

Below are a few basic questions you can ask to get started:

+ Where were you born and raised?
+ Do you have living parents or siblings?
+ What's your best childhood memory?
+ What's your most embarrassing moment?
+ What is your favorite food, color, and/or movie?
+ Why did you choose to be a marine?
+ Whom do you admire most in your life?

Why Would Anyone Care about My Story?

There is power in telling your story. Sharing your experiences, challenges, and yes, even failures, serves as a reminder that at one point or another we all experience hardships. You will find that you connect with others on a deeper level. Here are three reasons why you should share your story:

1. *Self-discovery through sharing.* Sharing personal experiences leads to awareness about deep-rooted issues you've been carrying. When you decide to tell your story, you'll feel that certain events might still sting quite a bit. Emotional sensitivity is an indicator that unresolved issues need addressing.

2. *Maintaining healthy personal and professional relationships.* Hardship shapes our personalities and perceptions more than we like to admit. For example, if you grew up

believing violence settles arguments, your reaction might be to get physical. Your story gives others tools to communicate with you in a positive and effective manner.

3. *Inspiration.* Sharing your story will inspire others to take action in their own lives. The fear (false evidence of appearing real) will diminish the more you share. You will inspire others to believe that anything is possible. They will adopt the motto, "If they can do it, so can I."

How to Share Your Story?

There are many ways that you can share your story. I'm an advocate of group discussions and journal writing. Whenever possible, share your story in person. Social media also provides the perfect audience, without boosting. If you aren't on Facebook, you can write it in a journal. Keep it short, sweet, and simple. Here are some tips to help you get started:

+ Social media. Post a snippet of your story on Facebook. Ask others to share their stories.
+ If you don't like to write, you can make a collage of pictures and captions. Instagram is a great outlet for this. You can even hash tag it (#MyMarineStory) and encourage others to do the same.
+ Make a video, add music, and post it on YouTube or Vimeo.

The most powerful tool we have in transforming our lives is to share our experiences. The path to transforming our life begins with self-discovery. The wound will only heal if you expose it. It's going to be painful at first, but once you get past the initial shock, you'll be fine. Understanding how experiences shape our personalities can help us with self-acceptance. Self-discovery is the first step in the path to self-acceptance.

CHAPTER 6

Define Culture, Values, and Mission

F OR THOSE OF YOU WHO struggle with the concept of divine guidance and higher purpose, I ask you to keep an open mind. Most people do not understand that there is a difference between religion and spirituality—yes, there is a difference.

Religion is an organized belief system in someone else's experience that incorporates rituals and customs to commemorate that individual's journey into divine awareness. Spirituality is exploring a variety of belief systems through your own experiences, so that you can help others change their lives in order to have positive outcomes. Religion focuses on practice, and spirituality is centered on action. They can coexist in the same state, but they are not the same.

But Gunny I'm Not a Spiritual Person

I've never met a Marine who doesn't believe in something. Even if you are an atheist, you believe in not believing; therefore, you believe in something. Spirituality is not about being religious. You can also take the best of both worlds, combine them to create a hybrid of beliefs, and tailor them to fit your life. It's about what works for you. Once the marine warrior understands that their essence and the spirit of the corps can coexist in perfect harmony, they can move past the demons that block their progression in fulfilling their destiny to serving our great nation honorably.

Establishing the Corps' Core Values

Every marine understands our institutional core values and the impact that they can have nationally and globally. The Marine Corps didn't always have a set of established values. In 1994, the Marine Corps noticed that the culture was changing rapidly. This would affect recruiting efforts and training. So, in order to understand what motivated generation X, they hired a team of experts (consisting of scientists, researchers, and psychologists) to figure it out. The team of experts discovered that generation X is driven by challenge, accountability, and ethics. Generation X wants to be held to a standard!

The 31st commandant general CC Krulak decided that it was time to establish institutional values. In addition to establishing the corps' core values, Krulak ordered that boot camp incorporate a culminating event that would test all of the training received in boot camp. In 1996, the culminating event was implemented and called "the crucible." The crucible marked the moment when the transformation was complete and a recruit became a marine, complete with an eagle, globe, and anchor ceremony and a warrior's breakfast. The official all marine message (ALMAR 439/96) was published, stating that honor, courage, and commitment would be known as our institutional corps' core values.

Marines Don't Do That!

General Leonard F. Chapman Jr., the 24th Commandant, wrote the following:

Marines don't wear a scruffy uniform.

Marines don't slouch around with their hands in their pockets.

Marines don't wear long hair.

Marines don't fail to respond with a "Yes, Sir" or "No, Sir" when speaking with a senior.

Marines don't render a halfhearted or sloppy salute to the Stars and Stripes or to their seniors.

Marines don't gang up on each other.

Marines don't question lawful orders.

Marines don't lie or cheat or break their word.

Marines don't abandon a fellow Marine in time of need.

Marines don't let down their fellow Marines by succumbing to drug temptation.

Marines don't meet problems with "It can't be done" or questions with the easy answer "No."

Marines don't knock the system without recommending appropriate change.

Marines don't (the list is endless) …

Marines do maintain their bearing.

Marines do more with less.

Marines do strive to improve themselves—physically, tactically, and intellectually.

Marines do honor their word.

Marines do set the example.

Marines do take initiative.

Marines do remain loyal to their families, fellow Marines, the Corps, and the Nation.

Marines do respect each other.

Marines do take care of each other.

Marines do what's right.

CHAPTER 7

Educate Your Team on Organizational Origins

H ISTORY IS AN IMPORTANT PART of marine culture, and we ensure that every marine understands that. No other branch of service places such emphasis on organizational history. By retelling our history, we answer the question, "Why?" The "why" defines our purpose as marines. The inspirational stories of our illustrious history have kept us alive for hundreds of years. Marines have assumed a place in history among some of the most legendary warriors, like Spartans and Vikings. Marines understand that our legacy can't survive if it's not retold to the next generation of marines. It's our responsibility and our duty to document our history, so that we can remember the greatest moments in our corps' history, therefore, reigniting esprit de corps. We must continue to seek opportunities to share these stories with others on our team.

Tun Tavern: The Masonic Lodge

Tun Tavern in Philadelphia, Pennsylvania, was established in 1682, by Samuel Carpenter. Tun Tavern was one of many uncharted Masonic lodges. Most unchartered lodges were clandestine, such as the one in Fredericksburg, Virginia, where General George Washington was made into a Freemason. In 1732 Saint John's No. 1 Lodge of the Grand Lodge of the Masonic Temple began at Tun Tavern, making it the birthplace of Masonic teachings in America. Freemasons like Benjamin Franklin and Thomas Jefferson gathered at Tun Tavern for meetings. In fact, Benjamin Franklin was the lodge's third grand master. Additionally, Robert Mullen, who is considered the Marine Corps' first recruiter, was the manager at Tun Tavern and rumored to have used Tun Tavern as a place to rally support for the American Revolution, while serving beers to patrons.

Freemasonry is a part of marine heritage. Freemasonry's influence in the Marine Corps is still present today. The use of symbols and a similar code of conduct leave traces of our connection to them. Their value system is the foundation for our corps' values of honor, courage, and commitment. Freemasons have occupied the ranks within the corps for years. Leaders such as Samuel Nicholas and John A. Lejeune were legendary Freemasons, who made valuable contributions to shaping our corps.

The City of Brotherly Love

Philadelphia comes from the Greek word phileo, which means brotherly love. The location inspires camaraderie, which is appropriate, considering it was the value system in the Marine Corps long before the corps' core values were officially established in 1996.

Brotherly/sisterly love begins in boot camp, which is also the beginning of esprit de corps. It's the kind of love that is soulful, and its expression depends on the soul of the one who bears it. It's honest and loyal and is intensified when marines undergo similar experiences, such as boot camp, field operations, and deployment.

We Have Two Birthdays

In ancient Egypt, a celebration was held on the day that a new pharaoh was crowned. The crowning of the pharaoh signified the transformation from man to god. The tradition led to a form of tribute to gods and goddesses by the Greek culture. From that point on, birthdays evolved into what they are today. Every marine can tell you the Marine Corps' birthday is November 10, 1775. It's one of the first dates a recruit learns at boot camp, and it becomes an important date for the rest of one's life. The day that you receive the sacred eagle, globe, and anchor isn't a day that marines forget—tired, hungry, smelly, feet blistered, and barely standing, but you were the happiest and proudest you've ever been in your life. It's engraved on your soul, and you're reborn as a marine. Forever you shall be a US Marine.

Marines should be aware that the Marine Corps birthday wasn't always the celebration we know it to be today. Therefore, it's essential that for as long as we live, no matter where we are, we celebrate the Marine Corps' birthday, every year just as we do our own. November 10, 1775 is not the only date that marks the creation of the Marine Corps. Below are a number of important dates in the evolution of the Marine Corp.

- 1775 November 10: Second Continental Congress authorizes the creation of two battalions of marines.
- 1793: Marine Corps is disbanded.
- 1794: Congress reactivates the navy, with five ships, and authorizes each ship to carry a complement of marines. Marines were on board ship under the command of the US Navy.
- 11 July 1798: Marine Corps is re-created and established as its own branch of service. Considered the Marine Corps' second birthday.
- 1921 October 21: Major General Edwin North McClellan suggests to the 13th Commandant, Major General John A. Lejeune, that November 10 officially be designated as the Marine Corps' birthday.
- 1921 November 1: General Lejeune sends out Marine Corps Order #47, which is known today as General John

A. Lejeune's Birthday Message. The message announces the official birthday and guidelines for marines.

+ 1921 November 10: Dinner is held in Washington, DC, to commemorate the Marine Corps' official birthdate.

+ 1923: The Marine Corps' birthday celebration is expanded and celebrated in various locations, in different ways: in Fort Mifflin, Pennsylvania, a dance is held at the barracks in the evening; in the Naval Yard in Norfolk, Virginia, a re-created battled is staged on the parade deck; at the naval station in Guantanamo Bay, Cuba, it's celebrated on November 12 with a field meet.

+ 1925: A "birthday ball" takes place. The unveiling of a tablet, at the Tun Tavern sight, establishes it as the Marine Corps' official birthplace.

+ 1935: The first cake-cutting ceremony takes place. The oldest and youngest marine custom origin is unknown.

+ 1951: A formal birthday ball pageant is held at Headquarters Marine Corps (HQMC), Marine Corps Base, Quantico, Virginia.

+ 1951 October 28: The Commandant requests that the Marine Corps' birthday ceremony be formalized throughout the Marine Corps.

+ 1956 January 26: The formalization of the Marine Corps' birthday ceremony is approved and includes the reading of General John A. Lejeune's birthday message, a cake-cutting ceremony, and other formalities, as outlined in the drill and ceremonies manual.

The Five W's and the How of Reflection

Recognizing the Marine Corps' birthdate and your own date of birth serves an important purpose in a marine's life. The celebration of both days allows us to reflect on our lives—our lives as individuals and as a part that serves the whole. The Marine Corps' birthday allows us to reflect on our legacy as an organization and also as marine leaders. It's the time to see where you are in accomplishing your personal and professional goals. These are what I call the "Five W's of and the How of Reflection": Why do you matter? What can you do better? Where are you lacking? Who can help you? When do you plan on doing this? How can you serve your marines better?

Ask your marines to write down their answers and sit down to discuss them one-on-one or as a group. It can really drive the point home. Just writing down the answer to these questions will provide insight to your personal and professional being.

- *Why do you matter?* We all have something to contribute to the whole. Battles aren't won by one marine but by teams that work in unison to accomplish the mission. Understanding how we contribute helps us create goals that align with the organization's values. Too often we get wrapped up in making the big green machine run and we forget how important we are. When we ask ourselves why we matter, we force ourselves to define our personal mission and how it relates to the big picture.

- *What can you do better?* No one is perfect—not even the meritorious marine or the sergeant who you've looked up to since you were a PFC. We need to get away from the expectation of perfection. Asking yourself what you can do better is not about focusing on your shortcomings; it's about focusing on areas that you have neglected and setting goals—for example, if you have been meaning to enroll in a college course but haven't.

- *Where are you lacking?* This question forces you to identify your shortcomings. It's not easy for marines to admit they aren't good at something. Remember that marines don't have weaknesses; we have things we aren't good at yet.

- *Who can help you?* No one has succeeded without help. Identify mentors that can assist in tightening up your shortcomings. All marines need a mentor. You can have as many as you like.

+ *When do you plan on doing this?* Create a plan to help keep you on track and focused. Be realistic when setting deadlines for accomplishing goals.

+ *How can you serve your marines better?* Don't forget that you serve your marines. If your reason for getting promoted is about making more money or so that you don't have to work, then you're wrong. The more rank you wear on your collar, the greater the responsibility you have to ensuring that your marines are taken care of.

CHAPTER 8

Determine How the Team Will Identify Themselves

WHY DOES FINDING AN IDENTITY for your team matter? In the book *Man and His Symbols*, Carl Yung explains that certain shapes and symbols have deeper meanings and affect our subconscious. Symbols are a way for humankind to express ideals or concepts that we can't understand. Additionally, Jung believed that there is a collective unconscious shared by humanity. For example, a cross symbolizes Christianity and the all-seeing eye found on the dollar bill represents higher knowledge and inner vision.

If we look at the symbolism in the eagle, globe, and anchor, we can it is filled with meaning. For example, stories of eagles are in almost every culture. The eagle represents a willingness to protect. The Chinese believe that the eagle is a sign of strength and courage. Celtic cultures see the eagle as protectors. The Greek used the symbol of the eagle to show leadership and as a sign of fertility. In Native American cultures, the eagle has magical powers and is one of the six directional guardians. You can take a combination of these meanings and apply them to the corps' emblem, reinforcing its meaning.

PERSPECTIVE	EAGLE	GLOBE	ANCHOR
PATRIOTIC	NATION	WORLDWIDE SERVICE	NAVAL TRADITIONS
ELEMENTAL	AIR	EARTH	WATER
RELIGIOUS	MESSENGER	HUMANITY	COMMITMENT

Perspective Chart

	CHARACTERISTICS
EAGLE	Nobility, Guardian. Angelic, Protector, Servant
GLOBE	Humanity, Souls of Mankind, Sacrifice in Service of Others
ANCHOR	Commitment, Dedication to Mission Accomplishment, Grounded

Emblem Characteristics

Exploring the meaning of the corps' emblem serves to strengthen it. Marines can use these meanings as a reminder of who we are and what we do as an organization.

Exercise: Create a Symbol

Symbols represent who we are and what we believe in. Without adding meaning to our symbols, we can't define a purpose. Determine what symbols matter to your team and why. What symbols represent who you are as a team and what your team philosophy is.

Why Is a Personalized Symbol So Important?

A personalized symbol represents who your team is, so that others will be able to identify you. When you have a mark that defines you, it reminds you and others of the values you have chosen to live by.

Ideas for Creating a Symbol

Have each member contribute to creating the team's identity. Each team member can contribute by doing the following:

1. Design a shield.
2. Pick four objects that have a personal meaning for you.
3. Write down what each of these items means to you. You can use historical references and meanings as well.
4. Make an electronic logo that you can add onto a team shirt, stickers, or other items.

Once you have created a symbol, your team should immediately begin using it as much as possible. As the team leader, jot down the day you began using it, and annotate how long it takes before others begin to associate the symbol with your team. This will allow you to gauge how much visibility your team is getting. Ensure that your symbol isn't offensive. Remember that it represents what you stand for, and you don't want negative attention associated with your team.

CHAPTER 9

Test the Team's Competence

Marine Warrior Ethos

ESPRIT DE CORPS IS ABOUT loyalty, faithfulness, and teamwork. It's no surprise that marines are known for this. They stick together and argue among each other like brothers and sisters, but let someone from the outside mess with one of us, and we will come at you like a pack of wolves—just like family. However, even in a family there are issues that must be worked through.

There are several steps to getting marines to come together, especially if there have been some trust issues in the past or you have a whole new section. Testing the limits of your team will allow you to uncover areas that need some tightening up. For example, your team may get along well but they aren't very good at finishing tasks in a timely manner. Or your team members have a hard time getting along, making getting things done impossible. You can continually test your marines to see what they are made of. Testing them will allow them to face fears head on, making them more confident.

Testing Your Team to Identify Shortcomings

1. Create a common hardship or an inspection that requires your team to work together. Physical fitness events (field

meets or friendly competitions) against other sections are a good place to start.

2. Create a common goal. Create something attainable the team can brag about achieving. If you decide to use a physical activity, ensure to establish a baseline in order to track progress.

3. Set guidelines. Let the team know what their left and right lateral limits are. For example, establish a time your team should finish an event or due date for tasks they're assigned as a team.

4. Let them fail. As long as there is no harm to your team or government property, this is okay. Failure is an essential part of growth. Additionally, it serves as a way to humble your team if they have started to get a bit too big for their britches.

5. Make recommendations for success, especially after the failure. Don't let your team fail without a debriefing on what they could have done better. Give them the opportunity to tell you what they could have done better. This will demonstrate that learning has occurred.

6. Praise in public and reprimand in private. Unless safety is involved, do this as a teaching point for all marines. Leaving the yelling to the drill instructors in boot camp. This will show them how to respect each other and set them up for how to address issues with their subordinates when they become team leaders.

7. Challenge them constantly: mentally, physically, emotionally, and spiritually. Don't forget to tell them when they have done a great job! This goes without saying.

Step 1: Create a Common Hardship

For starters, give them a challenge. As Mark Twain once said, "It's not the size of the dog in a fight; it's the size of the fight in the dog!" You can start off small and increase the difficultly to get them warmed up. This will allow them to see each other's strengths and shortcomings. Marines don't have weaknesses—we just have things we aren't good at yet! It's a proven fact that marines love to brag about completing the most difficult task. Marines don't like to do things the easy way. As a matter of fact, I think they kind of get a kick out of doing things the hard way. The harder the obstacle or task, the bigger the bragging rights and the ego.

In 2011, fresh off Marine Corps Recruit Depot at Parris Island, after a tour as a drill instructor and drill instructor school squad instructor, I was tasked with establishing the 1st Marine Logistics Group Corporals' Leadership Course. I think the sergeant major could still smell the squad bay stench on my uniform. No formal guidance was given, and I was sent on a Message to Garcia mission. I had no idea what I was about to get myself into.

Itching to drill and make corrections, I excitedly accepted. (Sucker!) This was not going to be an easy task, but I was so honored to have been asked to do this. A few days into my mission to launch the best Corporals' Leadership Course that Marine Corps Base Camp Pendleton has seen, I realized that we had no funding. The sergeant major knew this, but he also knew that I would find a way to make it happen. Challenge accepted.

Step 2: Create a Common Goal

The challenges kept coming. I didn't have the luxury of individually selecting my staff, and three marines (one staff sergeant and two sergeants) showed up at my office ready to train corporals, expect they were hardly presentable themselves. I could have ripped their alphas to shreds, but there was too much work that needed to be done. The Marine Corps Base Camp Pendleton Corporals' Leadership Course had a reputation for being one of the best leadership courses for small unit leaders. I was determined to make our Corporals' Course legendary, and they were going to help me do it.

By giving your marines a goal, they have something to focus on.

Ensure that it is attainable and appropriate—and not illegal. Don't set your marines up for failure by having them do something that compromises their integrity and bring discredit to the unit and the Marine Corps. Ensure that you emphasize that they will fail and succeed together. There is no individual glory.

Step 3: Set Guidelines

In the weeks that followed, I set the ground rules. Show time was 0600, ready for physical training (PT); hygiene time was thirty minutes, and they needed to catch breakfast on the run, because there would be no time for a leisurely warrior's breakfast. Early mornings and late nights would ensure success! I trained my staff hard.

We went on boots and uts runs, did uniform inspections, practiced guidon and sword manual, and my favorite, drilled every day. By the end of the first week, my staff hated me and wanted transfers back to their units. Finally, I sat them down and explained to them that this was necessary if we were going to train our corporals better than the base's course. They toughed it out, but they were not happy.

Marines have a love—hate relationship with rules and standards. We love reaping the benefits that come with upholding standards, but we struggle doing it. When your marines first begin working together, they aren't going to like all of the new rules. Who does? But it is necessary in order to establish a routine and the expectation. They will moan and groan. It's okay to hear them out. But adjustments should not be made until the team has proven they can weather the storm and performs to the standard. After about four weeks, you can adjust if you need to, but only for small tweaks and if absolutely necessary.

Step 4: Let Them Fail

Pick-up day was getting closer, and I felt that my staff wasn't ready. We had only covered the guidon and sword manual portion of drill, and we hadn't even gotten into how to teach and grade drill; they could barely run PT from the PT table. The day came, and on the very first PT session, my sergeant was a hot mess. He forgot to have them form for PT, the warm-up was out of sequence, and his counting cadence was off. I cringed through the entire thing. I watched as he fell flat on his sword.

After the end of the day, I pulled them in and asked them what we could have done better. They looked at me in disbelief, and without saying a word, they knew that they had been wrong for complaining about training them so hard.

I looked at them and said, "Do I need to say it, or do you all know what I am about to say?"

One of the young sergeants looked at me and said, "This is why you wanted us to keep practicing, so this wouldn't happen!" I nodded yes.

Watching your marines fail isn't easy. And failure is okay, as long as it's in a training environment and there isn't a safety risk. What isn't okay is not trying again. When your marines fail, they are going to be depressed. They will feel the sting of their own failure without you having to say, "I told you so." But it's important to let them go through with this because failure is an essential part of growth. Without failure, we can't assess our limitations. Additionally, it's a great humbling technique, especially for those marines who are a little too big for their britches.

Step 5: Make Recommendations for Success, Especially After the Failure

The only thing that I borrowed from the Marine Corps Base Camp Pendleton Corporals' Leadership Course was the curriculum skeleton. And after reviewing it, I realized that there was no drill and no guidon and sword manual instruction in the curriculum; adjustments needed to be made. I was shocked! How could this be? How could corporals attend a course without drill? I went to the sergeant major and asked him if he would approve adding drill to the curriculum. Of course, he didn't have an issue with it, as long as the curriculum hours remained the same and they had ample time for chow. No problem—done!

Step 6: Praise in Public and Reprimand in Private

Most young non commissioned officers (NCOs) believe that if they act like their drill instructors, they will elicit that same response from those they lead. I used to believe that too. Our young marines need to keep in mind that the drill instructor has one objective-to make you into a United States Marine. As a leader of Marines (outside of boot camp), you have many objectives.

I finally realized that being a drill instructor 24-7 wasn't a good idea when I watched how my young NCOs in our new and improved Corporals' Leadership Course were treating each other. It wasn't quite what I had envisioned. NCOs walked around making corrections that were not only embarrassing, but also uncalled for. Don't get me wrong; I am not saying that you have to be soft spoken or hand out hugs during chow. I am saying that you should treat others how you would like to be treated and be firm, fair, and consistent.

Step 7: Challenge them Constantly.

Stagnation kills and movement means life. When marines get bored, they get into trouble. If you are constantly introducing them to something new, they will grow to be well rounded and grounded. Marines will complain about having to do something new, but you will see that after a while they will appreciate that you have taken the time to expose them to something they would have not otherwise been exposed to.

I can remember when it was difficult to get young NCOs to come to our Corporals" course. Marines complained and I swear that a few had to be dragged down to our building by their Staff Non Commissioned Officer (SNCO). But after they graduated and bragged how they survived being under the evil Gunnery Sergeant Mendoza, we had marines lining up for the next class. Marines want to be challenged. It's bred into us in boot camp.

CHAPTER 10

Keep Your Marines Inspired

A S US MARINES, WE HAVE been bestowed the privilege of protecting our great nation. More importantly, we have the scope of direct influence to transform people's lives within its ranks. We are inspired by the amazing stories from the heroes within its ranks, conspiracies, and sightings of guardian angels.

Tradition is relayed through the stories we tell, but they also define who we are. Marine Corps commercials depict ordinary men performing extraordinary feats, such as climbing volcanoes and slaying dragons; they reveal that we are more than just mere mortals. Marines are extraordinary! A young man who can climb a mountain and defeat the mythical creature is rewarded by being transformed into a marine warrior.

The mythical creature represents many things to many marines. It could be the obstacles that they had to overcome—maybe fear of leaving home for the first time—or the overwhelming sense of responsibility to succeed. We all have those demons within us. To overcome these demons, many of us accepted the challenge to become marines, hoping to obtain the secret formula, to tap into our inner power.

The Marine Corps wasn't always admired like it is today. If you have ever read *First to Fight* by Lieutenant General Victor A. Krulak, USMC (Retired), you know that many attempts had been made to disband the Marine Corps. Some of those attempts were made by influential officers in the US Army. With the Marine Corps around, the US Army couldn't gain the respect and admiration that its service members hoped for.

Born only a few months after the army, the Marine Corps has proven to be a different breed. Even though the Marine Corps is smaller in every facet, from personnel to the allotted yearly budget it receives, it always finds a way to accomplish the mission and look good doing it. I think what really pisses the US Army off is that the Marine Corps does more with less——every time! It is obvious that the Marine Corps is Uncle Sam's (favorite) misguided child. At one point, the other branches of services joked that USMC stood for Uncle Sam's Misguided Children. The funny thing is, marines embraced it.

The Titanic Sinks to Save the Marine Corps

In 1912 an army officer named Archibald Butt was almost successful in disbanding the Marine Corps. Major Archibald Butt was a journalist in the US Army before being assigned to the White House to serve as a military aide under two presidential administrations. Butt was a very skilled writer and an even better communicator. His writing skills earned him praise and recognition, and in 1909 he was asked to serve under President William Taft. It was during this time that Butt had the most influence at the White House.

Butt attempted to join the Marine Corps, prior to being commissioned in the US Volunteers, which was controlled by the army. The Marine Corps refused to commission Butt because of rumors surrounding his sexual preference for men. Politics played a huge role, just as it does today. The reason for the rumors was partly because Butt was not married and was known to have never made any marriage proposals to available women. Butt believed the rumors were started by a marine he had crossed.

Keep in mind that there wasn't much room to deviate from societal norms, as there is today, and reputation was everything. Butt was furious and vowed revenge. Sure enough, as Butt made his way to the top, he began to embed subtle messages about disbanding the Marine Corps in the ears of powerful men, such as the president. Upon serving his second tour under another US President, Butt was determined to get rid of the Marine Corps. However, fate had a different plan in mind.

On March 1, 1912, Butt boarded the RMS *Titanic* to take a long-needed vacation, and it sank on April 14, 1912. Major Butt's body was never recovered. Regardless of whether the story is true, it has received some delightful embellishments throughout its lifetime. There are three facts that stand: (1) Major Butt did die, (2) the *Titanic* did sink, and (3) the Marine Corps is still alive today.

What Is in a Name?

An old sergeant major of mine used to say that you had two names: one was United States Marine, which was earned in boot camp, and the other was your surname bestowed upon you after birth. As a marine, your name signifies a long legacy of two bloodlines. A good exercise to do with your team is to have them research the history of their birth name and surname and give a presentation to the team. Not only will it bring insight to the team about where their family came from, but the individual might learn something they didn't know.

Lucy Brewer

Marines come in all shapes and sizes. The Marine Corps isn't just a gun club for boys but is also a club for badass girls. The story of Lucy Brewer serves as a reminder that women have made significant contributions. Who was Lucy Brewer? Lucy was Louise Baker, was a farm girl from Plymouth, Massachusetts. Her story was inspired by a woman who is reported to have joined the Marines Corps and served on the USS Constitution. Supposedly, Lucy moved to Boston and was befriended by a woman that owned a brothel. Unbeknownst to Lucy, the life she was about to enter was a life of slavery as a prostitute—but Lucy refused to accept that fate. According to legend, Lucy joined the Marine Corps by pretending to be a man and was deployed on the USS Constitution during the War of 1812.

What is interesting about Lucy's story is that the only statement that the Marine Corps made about the validity of the story was that the enlistment process and berthing accommodations aboard ship would have made it impossible for her to hide her gender. If the story of Lucy Brewer were true, would that change how successful the Marine Corps has been? Of course it wouldn't. And why can't we believe that the legend of Lucy Brewer is true? She is one example of how many women escape similar circumstances by forging their own destinies, and also a reminder of how many women don't escape that fate and are forced to live as sex slaves.

As a drill instructor on Parris Island, I saw this more than once. Women enlisted in order to escape an awful future. Why wouldn't the Marine Corps recognize and allow a woman with such courage and conviction to be a part of our illustrious history? Is it because they do not want to admit that it is possible that a woman could have fooled their recruiters, or maybe because it would be a liability? Nonetheless, Lucy reminds us that anything is possible if we put our minds to it.

You can use this story as the introduction to an exercise that has them identify someone that overcame the odds and made a significant impact. Ask them to identify three characteristics that they admire about the person and how they plan on modeling those characteristics.

Tap Code Team-Building Exercise

Just as symbols express concepts that we cannot understand, music speaks what cannot be expressed. You can even go as far as designating a theme song for your team. Music is the guiding light through the darkness. It heals the soul and reawakens the spirit. The Greek philosopher Pythagoras described music as a series of calculated vibrations. He believed that the secret of the universe could be revealed through numbers. But more significantly, each number had its own meaning and vibration. Pythagoras's teachings tell us that there are nine numbers and vibrations that govern the universe.

The use of "tap code" is an excellent example of Pythagoras's theory. But the tap code is rarely used today by marines. Although its origins can be dated back to Ancient Greece, the tap code was most commonly used by marine and sailor prisoners of war (POWs) during the Vietnam Conflict. There are countless stories of how the tap code made the lives of POWs bearable. Some POWs give credit to the tap code for being the hope that they held onto until they were released or rescued.

Teaching your marines how to use the tap code can be used as a team building exercise. But what is the tap code? It is a method used to transmit messages through a series of taps. Each letter in the alphabet corresponds to a number in a row and column in a five-by-five grid. The first tap designates the row, which is horizontal, and the second tap is the column, which is vertical. There are a series of pauses between each letter in order to be able to distinguish when a new letter is being transmitted.

Taps	1	2	3	4	5
1	A	B	C/K	D	E
2	F	G	H	I	J
3	L	M	N	O	P
4	Q	R	S	T	U
5	V	W	X	Y	Z

Tap Code

The Marine and Saint Michael

The Battle of Chosin Reservoir in 1950 is considered to be one of the battles that defined the marines' invincible spirit and forged a brotherhood whose sacrifices will never be forgotten. With documented temperatures between twenty and thirty degrees below zero, the marines of 1st Marine Division were up against some pretty impossible odds. The commander of Fox Company, Captain Will Barber, was ordered to take his company of 240 marines to Toktong Pass and protect it at all costs. The marines would protect an escape route deep in the Nangnim Mountains for General MacArthur's United Nation Forces. The orders were given with the final stated "at all costs."

Surrounded by 120,000 Korean and Chinese Communist Forces (CCF), Fox Company would not only be up against the enemy forces, but also the unforgiving weather and terrain. The enemy was set on the annihilation of the 1st Marine Division. However, Fox Company put up a good fight. Although Captain Barber was wounded in both legs, he ordered that two marines carry him around on a stretcher so that he could encourage his marines to fight harder. And harder they fought. Captain Barber lost twenty marines and fifty-four were wounded, but Fox Company managed to take down over five hundred CCF. Marines consider themselves to be invincible, protected by guardian angels during firefights. Captain Barber would probably attest to that now, looking back at the situation.

There is one story of a young US Marine who was forward deployed to Korea. He wrote a letter to his mother about a spiritual experience that took place during the war. No one knows if it was it the battle at Chosin Reservoir, but what is known is that the story circulated for many years after it first appeared. The marine had been injured during a firefight and survived the ordeal. He believed he had survived because he received assistance from a heavenly guardian, Archangel Michael, also known as Saint Michael in the Catholic religion. Archangel Michael is known for casting Lucifer out of heaven during the battle between heaven and hell. He's also known to be made in God's image and is considered the leader of God's angelic army.

The letter that the young marine wrote to his mother somehow found its way to a US Navy Chaplain, Father Walter Muldy. Father Muldy was so moved by the events that he personally interviewed the young marine and the marine's platoon sergeant. After obtaining pertinent details about the event, he obtained permission from the marine's mother to use the letter. In 1951, Father Muldy retold the story to five thousand marines at a naval base in San Diego, California, where he had been invited to speak. The popularity of the letter grew so much that it was retold on the radio for eight years during Christmas.[7] Playing the broadcast[8] is a great way to instill motivation, especially if it is used as a tie in about the Battle of Chosin Reservoir.

---

[7] https://www.tfpstudentaction.org/resources/prayers-for-students/incredible-miracle-u-s-Marine-saved-by-saint-michael-1. Accessed April 3, 2017.

[8] https://www.youtube.com/watch?v=7FCVco1weHU. Accessed April 3, 2017.

God Created Marines on the Eighth Day

In the beginning was the word, and the word was God. All else was darkness and void. So, God created the heavens and the earth. He created the sun and the moon and the stars, so that light might penetrate the darkness. The Earth, God divided between the land and the sea, and these He filled with many assorted creatures. [9]

On the fourth day, in a happy mood, God made creatures of the land; God called them soldiers. With a twinkle in His eye and a smile on His face, God made their trousers too baggy and placed covers on their heads that looked like baseball caps. He also made their pockets oversized, so that they may warm their cold hands. And to adorn their uniforms, God gave them many badges that they could earn later. He gave them emblems and crests and all sorts of shiny things that glittered, and devices that dangled, that looked like flare from a TGIF waitress's uniform. Nonetheless, they carried out God's orders in unique fashion. Often deviating from the plan, but adjusting on the fly, they were successful from time to time.

The dark, salty, slimy creatures that inhabited the murky depths of the oceans, God called sailors, and He provided them with ships to float above sea. He dressed them accordingly, after getting carried away with the land creatures. They had tiny trousers that looked like bells at the bottom, and their shirts had cute little flaps; they wore funny-looking Dixie-cup hats. He gave them long sideburns and nicknamed them "squids." He banished them to a lifetime at sea, to keep sea demons from crawling onto the Earth.

On the sixth day God thought about creating some air creatures for which he designed a Greyhound bus driver's uniform. He discarded this idea during the first week, and it was not until years later that some apostles revived this idea and established what we now know as the "wild blue yonder wonders."

And on the seventh day, as you know, God rested.

---

[9]   Adapted and modified from Genesis 1:1, The Bible, King James Version.

But on the eighth day at 0430, before the sun was up, God looked down upon Earth and felt something was missing. So He thought about His labors, and in His divine wisdom, God created a godlike creature from fire, air, and the very fuel-energy of the universe. And these creatures, who God created in His own image, were to relay messages back and forth between God and mankind. They would have no boundaries. They were to be the guardians of the air, the land, and the sea. And these He gave uniforms that made them invincible, so they could wage war against the forces of evil. Some were green, some were tan, and some were blue with red trim. He gave them a magical seal that would distinguish them from the rest. And this seal the godlike creatures proudly tattooed on their chest. He gave them fighting spirits and adorned these creatures with wings, which earth beings called "white sleeves." He gave them the ability to withstand an insurmountable amount of pain and to have compassionate hearts. And He made these creatures smart but also gave them swords to use as a last resort.

And at the end of the eighth day, God looked down upon the Earth, upon all His labors, and saw that it was good. But he still did not have a name for His last creation. He thought and thought. These marvelous creatures were His greatest creation, and they deserved more than just a name—they deserved a title. And so He honored them by calling them *marines*!

CHAPTER 11

The Keeper of the Flame

F IRE IS ONE OF THE universal elements of the world, along with air, wind, water, and earth. Because fire can be both a cleansing and destructive force, it is considered to be from a divine origin. In many cultures, fire represents God, and references of fire appear repeatedly throughout the Bible. In Africa there are villages that have altars dedicated to sacred fire, which serve to unify the people of the nation. The Zoroastrian religion built fire temples, in which their followers took the sacred flame with them. The sacred flame reminds us of our faith in the organization and to each other, that we may continue the legacy by igniting the fire in each generation of marines.

The Keeper of the Sacred Flame

The "keeper of the flame" is a phrase that I have heard on and off throughout my Marine Corps career. I can recall the old, crusty gunnery sergeants telling us that someday we would be the keepers and have to keep the flame alive. At the time I didn't fully understand what that responsibility entailed. But once I became a seasoned sergeant, I began to understand that it was my responsibility to maintain traditions and uphold the standards. Sergeant Major Kent, sergeant major of the Marine Corps in 2008, revived that concept for me when he released a memorandum in which he stated, "SNCO's and NCO's are the keepers of tradition and standards!" He didn't state that it was an officer's responsibility; he stated that it was up to the SNCO's and NCO's to do it.

The keeper of the flame is the person in the unit who upholds the standards, traditions, and customs of the Marine Corps. They are usually the marine most aligned with the organization's mission and vision. The keeper of the organization is passionate and keeps the Marine Corps focused on the priorities. Additionally, they ensure that they foster an environment where others in the organization can develop as a result of their leadership.

I have spent years working on self–mastery of life and made the Marine Corps a part of my life path, not just something to do from 9:00 a.m. to 5:00 p.m. each day. It's because of the SNCOs and NCOs that our traditions are still alive. Granted, officers such as General John A. Lejeune made them official, but it has been the enlisted marine who has carried out those orders.

The Keeper of the Flame

Who am I?

I am the keeper of the flame.

I wear two names on my uniform: one is the name of the family that I was born into and the other is the name of the family that I earned the right to be a part of.

The eagle, globe, and anchor that I wear over my chest are imprinted on my soul. The symbols represent the name of every United States Marine who has served to protect our nation.

I am the keeper of the flame.

I will never forget the sacrifices of those before me, because they are the ember that burns bright. I vow to remember them and to strive to emulate their honorable actions.

I am the keeper of the flame.

I believe in the Mighty Spirit, the corps, the marines I serve with, and preserving our corps' legacy. I will make every effort to nourish the flame within me and within every marine under my charge.

I cannot be destroyed, even after my physical body is gone. I will continue to live on so as long the ember continues to burn bright.

Final Words

Each marine follows four mottos: 1) esprit de corps; 2) discipline and spirit; 3) *ductus exemplo*; and 4) *spiritus invictus*. Each motto explains an aspect of marine life that serves as guidance for how we should live our lives. "Esprit de corps" provides insight to the unique connection that all marines have to each other and the organization. "Discipline and spirit" reveals the foundation instilled in every marine, from the time they step foot on the yellow footprints. "*Ductus exemplo*" outlines the importance of leading by example. And "*spiritus invictus*" is the unrelenting spirit marines have to overcome adversity. The four mottos are broken into four books of wisdom. Each book describes the symbolism, myth, and magic that bring to life the essence of the motto.

Esprit de Corps is book one of four in the *Core Values Series*. Esprit de corps is represented by a circle. We can't win battles alone. The circle symbolizes the team, in unity, acting as one. The color associated with camaraderie is red for the blood that our fellow brothers and sisters have shed on the battlefield. It reminds us that without one another, we can't defeat the enemy. Therefore, we must build a foundation and strengthen the connections we have within our team, to overcome evil. The spirit animal that governs esprit de corps is the wolf. The wolf makes cooperation a priority over competition. Furthermore, the wolf is a pack animal and understands the benefits to running with a pack. The wolf exudes quiet confidence and can be compassionate and loving, but if there is trouble near, he or she will do whatever it takes to protect the pack.

Back in 1775,
My Marine Corps came alive.
First there came the color red,
To show the world the blood we shed.
Then there came the color gold,
To show the world that we are bold.
Then there came the color blue,
To show the world that we are true.
Last there came the color black,
To show the world that we are back![10]

---

[10]   Marine Corps running cadence.

The Marine's Prayer

ALMIGHTY FATHER, WHOSE COMMAND IS over all and whose love never fails, make me aware of Thy presence and obedient to Thy will. Keep me true to my best self, guarding me against dishonesty in purpose and deed and helping me to live so that I can face my fellow marines, my loved ones, and Thee without shame or fear. Protect my family. Give me the will to do the work of a marine and to accept my share of responsibilities with vigor and enthusiasm. Grant me the courage to be proficient in my daily performance. Keep me loyal and faithful to my superiors and to the duties my country and the Marine Corps have entrusted to me. Make me considerate of those committed to my leadership. Help me to wear my uniform with dignity, and let it remind me daily of the traditions which I must uphold. If I am inclined to doubt, steady my faith; if I am tempted, make me strong to resist; if I should miss the mark, give me courage to try again. Guide me with the light of truth and grant me wisdom by which I may understand the answer to my prayer. Amen.

About the Author

J OANNA MENDOZA IS A RETIRED US Marine, who has deployed all over the world, to include multiple combat tours to Iraq and Afghanistan. She has served as a Drill Instructor, Drill Instructor-Instructor, and as a Sergeant Instructor. JoAnna holds a BA in Intelligence Studies, and a Certification in Strength and Conditioning Training. Additionally, she has attended various military schools, such as: Combat Life Saver, Marine Corps Martial Arts Black Belt, Formal Instructor, Curriculum Developer, Substance Abuse Control Officer, Suicide Prevention Officer, Uniformed Victim Advocate, Marine Corps Special Operations Training Course, and various leadership academies.

As a Drill Instructor she changed lives. As an instructor at Drill Instructor School, one of the most esteemed schools, in the Marine Corps, she impacted the future of the Marine Corps, by directly influencing how Marine Drill Instructors transformed selected men and women into Marines. Her passion and can-do-attitude are a result of overcoming challenges in her personal and professional life.

As a self-proclaimed advocate for underrepresented populations, she consistently strives to bring awareness to issues within our society. Whether, it's through, sharing personal experiences, direct connections, social networking sites, or through writing, she is committed to providing insight, information and resources to help those in need. She believes that each one of us is on a mission to find a unique gift to share with the world that will make it a better place. No gift is too big, or too small.

JoAnna continues to inspire people wherever she goes. After the Marine Corps, it was important for her to secure a position that would allow her to make a difference. Currently, she works for an agency that allows her to assist others provide safe and loving homes for children and adults with special needs. JoAnna is a single mother and her son, Aidan, is her pride and joy. They currently live in the beautiful Arizona desert.

Printed in the United States
By Bookmasters